LUNAR NEW YEAR

THIS EDITION
Produced for DK by WonderLab Group LLC
Jennifer Emmett, Erica Green, Kate Hale, *Founders*

Editor Maya Myers; **Photography Editor** Nicole DiMella; **Managing Editor** Rachel Houghton;
Designers Project Design Company; **Researcher** Michelle Harris;
Copy Editor Lori Merritt; **Indexer** Connie Binder; **Proofreader** Susan K. Hom;
Series Reading Specialist Dr. Jennifer Albro; **Sensitivity Reader** Marie Tang

First American Edition, 2025
Published in the United States by DK Publishing, a division of Penguin Random House LLC
1745 Broadway, 20th Floor, New York, NY 10019

Copyright © 2025 Dorling Kindersley Limited
25 26 27 28 29 10 9 8 7 6 5 4 3 2 1
001–349521–Sep/2025

All rights reserved.
Without limiting the rights under the copyright reserved above, no part of this publication may be reproduced, stored in or introduced into a retrieval system, or transmitted, in any form, or by any means (electronic, mechanical, photocopying, recording, or otherwise), without the prior written permission of the copyright owner.

DK values and supports copyright. Thank you for respecting intellectual property laws by not reproducing, scanning or distributing any part of this publication by any means without permission. By purchasing an authorised edition, you are supporting writers and artists and enabling DK to continue to publish books that inform and inspire readers. No part of this publication may be used or reproduced in any manner for the purpose of training artificial intelligence technologies or systems. In accordance with Article 4(3) of the DSM Directive 2019/790, DK expressly reserves this work from the text and data mining exception.

Published in Great Britain by Dorling Kindersley Limited

A catalog record for this book is available from the Library of Congress.
HC ISBN: 979-8-2171-2544-9
PB ISBN: 979-8-2171-2543-2

DK books are available at special discounts when purchased in bulk for sales promotions, premiums, fund-raising, or educational use.
For details, contact:
DK Publishing Special Markets, 1745 Broadway, 20th Floor, New York, NY 10019
SpecialSales@dk.com

Printed and bound in China
Super Readers Lexile® levels 500L to 610L
Lexile® is the registered trademark of MetaMetrics, Inc. Copyright © 2024 MetaMetrics, Inc. All rights reserved.

The publisher would like to thank the following for their kind permission to reproduce their images:
a=above; c=center; b=below; l=left; r=right; t=top; b/g=background
Alamy Stock Photo: Eddie Gerald 21cl, Imago / Xinhua / Wang Song 12cb, Steve Lillie 12b, ZUMA Press Inc / Ivan Abreu / SOPA Images 18t; **Dreamstime.com:** Antoniosantosg 9, Design56 29tl, Jessica Girvan 17br, Golfxx 18crb, Keechuan 27tl, Msphotographic 14br, Phive2015 30, Ronniechua 19crb, Xiaoyong 11b; **Getty Images:** AFP / Johannes Eisele 28, KIM JAE-HWAN / AFP 25tr, Anadolu / Ihsaan Haffejee 26cl, Archive Photos / Hulton Archive 14tl, Evans / Three Lions 15, Mint Images 21br, NurPhoto / Ronen Tivony 24, Robertus Pudyanto 27br; **Getty Images / iStock:** Prapat Aowsakorn 4-5, Dole08 14crb, DragonImages 7b, E+ / hxyume 3, E+ / KSChong 7cra, E+ / SolStock 22, jethuynh 16-17, lusea 13, yipengge 29crb; **Shutterstock.com:** Ariadna22822 26, BananaHub 29t, jieyu16 23bl, Lanlana839 1, leungchopan 21tr, Niny2405 11tr, Ekaterina Pokrovsky 6bl, PR Image Factory 20, Jeong-Seon 25bl, Huy Thoai 8

Cover images: *Front:* **Dreamstime.com:** Atorn Buaksantiah (gold); **Getty Images / iStock:** E+ / RichLegg;
Shutterstock.com: dokodoko tr, Sensvector (background); *Back:* **Dreamstime.com:** Diana Vasileva

www.dk.com

This book was made with Forest Stewardship Council™ certified paper – one small step in DK's commitment to a sustainable future.
Learn more at www.dk.com/uk/information/sustainability

Level 2

LUNAR NEW YEAR

Emma Carlson Berne

Contents

6	Welcoming Spring
10	A Moon and a Beast
16	Color and Light
20	Getting Ready
22	Let's Eat!

24	Celebrations Around the World
28	Night of Light
30	Glossary
31	Index
32	Quiz

Welcoming Spring

Dancers swirl in red and gold. They carry a giant dragon puppet through the streets. The puppet's rippling body dances on sticks. Musicians bang drums. People shout and cheer. Community groups carry flags and wave to the crowds. Everyone is celebrating Lunar New Year.

Communities and families celebrate Lunar New Year around the world. They hold festivals. They decorate and clean their houses. They prepare special meals. Together, they mark the end of one year and the beginning of another.

Ho Chi Minh City, Vietnam

Lunar New Year is also called the Spring Festival or Chinese New Year. The holiday lasts for 15 days. It falls in the late winter. It's time to welcome spring. This is a time to celebrate and be with family.

For some families, Lunar New Year is one of the most important holidays of the year. Huge celebrations are held in China, North Korea, South Korea, Malaysia, Vietnam, and Singapore. Asian communities outside Asia also come together to celebrate.

A Moon and a Beast

Lunar New Year has been celebrated for almost 3,500 years. For much of that time, China used a lunisolar calendar. This calendar follows the movements of the sun and the moon. A new month began when a new moon was in the sky. Lunar New Year began on the first day of the first month of the year.

Today, most countries use the Western or Gregorian calendar. But the Lunar New Year date still comes from the lunisolar calendar. So, the holiday falls on different dates on the Western calendar each year.

A full moon over Shanghai, China

11

People often tell this legend to explain the holiday.

Long ago, there was a beast named Nian. Nian means "year." Nian would eat people's animals and crops on the night before the new year. To make Nian go away, people set food in front of their doors.

Then, a wise man realized that Nian was afraid of the color red. People started putting red decorations in front of their doors. They stayed awake at night to fight him off. Nian was afraid of loud noises, too. People lit firecrackers to scare Nian. They still do today!

San Francisco, California, 1945

Hundreds of years ago, people began gathering for feasts during Lunar New Year. They cleaned the house to sweep away bad luck. They stayed up all night to welcome the new year.

Symbolic Snacks

People buy special snacks during Lunar New Year. These foods can symbolize different things.

DRIED LONGANS (a type of fruit): Reunion with loved ones

CANDIES AND SWEETS: A sweet life

PEANUTS: Vitality and long life

Over time, celebrations became more elaborate. People built big dragon puppets for parades. They sewed new clothes. Families bought candied fruits, seeds, and nuts. They made special dumplings that were made to look like boat-shaped pieces of money. In 1949, the Chinese government renamed the event. Spring Festival became an official national holiday.

Hong Kong, around 1956

Color and Light

Boom! Boom! Here comes the parade! It is colorful and noisy. Giant puppets float down the street.

Ho Chi Minh City, Vietnam

Look at these huge lions! Each one has two people inside. They make the lion dance. The lion dancers visit businesses and restaurants. They dance for the people working there.

Feeding the Lion

Restaurant owners may "feed" the lion! They cut up a head of lettuce or cabbage. The lion "eats" the lettuce. Then, it spits it back out! This symbolizes the spreading of wealth.

Flower market in Hong Kong

Special street markets sell flowers, fruit, and sweets. Some markets stay open all night. Shoppers buy oranges and other fruits. These fruits are symbols of good luck.

Buying flowers and plants is important, too. They stand for growth in the new year.

Parents and older relatives give younger family members red envelopes. The envelopes are filled with money.

And there's no bedtime! Staying awake all night is a tradition.

Red Envelopes

Children often receive red envelopes on Lunar New Year. The envelopes symbolize good luck in the coming year. It's important to show good manners when accepting an envelope. Take it with both hands. Thank the giver. And don't open it in public!

Getting Ready

Cleaning the house is an important part of preparing for Lunar New Year celebrations. People think of sweeping out last year's bad luck.

The house is clean. It's time to decorate! Many Lunar New Year decorations are red. Red stands for happiness and good luck. People make red paper decorations. Some even paint their front doors red. Stay away, Nian!

Stop That Broom!

People don't do any cleaning on the first day of Lunar New Year. They might sweep away the New Year's good luck!

Let's Eat!

It's the eve of the first day of the holiday. Families gather for a special meal. They welcome relatives who have traveled from far away.

The table is spread with food. The foods symbolize good luck and happiness. Some families serve a whole fish. The fish stands for abundance, or having more than enough. People serve dumplings, which also mean plenty. The dumplings may be filled with meat and vegetables. Sweet cake made from rice flour might be on the New Year table. Another dessert is called Eight Treasure Rice. It's decorated with eight kinds of fruits and candies. Yum!

Celebrations Around the World

Communities around the world celebrate Lunar New Year. In Los Angeles, California, Asian-American communities hold a big parade. More than 100,000 people come out to watch!

In South Korea, some families dress in traditional outfits called hanbok. Younger people bow in front of elders. They offer good wishes. Elders offer blessings. They give gifts of money. Some families cook a soup called tteokguk [DUCK-gook]. The soup has long rice cakes. Tteokguk symbolizes new beginnings and a long life.

In South Africa, people visit a large temple. There, they pray. They watch a traditional dance. The dragon puppet swirls and leaps.

FGS Nan Hua Temple, Bronkhorstspruit, South Africa

Symbolic Foods

In Malaysia, families often eat a cold dish of chopped raw fish. It's served with pickled vegetables and sauces. These foods stand for abundance.

In Indonesia, people visit temples. The temples are decorated with lanterns and candles—red, of course! The Grebeg Sudiro festival celebrates Javanese and Chinese cultures. People offer food to a watching crowd. The crowd devours the cakes, fruits, and vegetables.

Solo City, Indonesia

Night of Light

The night streets are lit with showers of sparks. Blacksmiths throw hot iron at a cold stone wall. Golden sparks spray out.

Nuanquan, Hebei Province, China

Kuala Lumpur, Malaysia

Tonight is the Lantern Festival. This is the last day of Lunar New Year. People fill the streets to watch parades. They eat sweet rice balls called tangyuan [TONG you-an].

Fancy lanterns are everywhere. Their light pushes back the darkness. They light the way to the new year to come.

Glossary

Abundance
A great supply, or plenty

Community
A group of people who live together or share common customs within a larger society

Dumpling
Dough stuffed with a filling of meat or vegetables and cooked

Elaborate
Complex, with lots of detail

Gregorian calendar
A calendar introduced in the late 1500s, in general use today

Javanese
Belonging to a native group of people living on the island of Java in Indonesia

Legend
A story from the past that is believed by many people, but is not proved to be true

Lunisolar
Relating to both the sun and the moon

Symbolize
To stand for or represent

Temple
A building used for worship or prayer

Traditional
Done the way people in a certain group have done something for a long time

Index

abundance 23, 27

cleaning 7, 14, 20–21

dragon puppets 6, 15, 26

dumplings 15, 23

firecrackers 13

fish 23, 27

foods 14, 15, 18, 22–23, 25, 27, 29

Lantern Festival 29

legend 12–13

lion puppets 16–17

lunisolar calendar 10–11

Nian (beast) 12–13, 21

parades 15, 16, 24, 29

red decorations 13, 21, 27

red envelopes 19

street markets 18

sweeping 14, 20, 21

symbolic foods 14, 23, 25, 27

temples 26, 27

world celebrations 9, 24–27

Quiz

Answer the questions to see what you have learned. Check your answers in the key below.

1. What is one other name for Lunar New Year?

2. True or False: Lunar New Year begins on the last day of the last month of the lunisolar calendar.

3. What does the name Nian mean?

4. What can serving a whole fish on Lunar New Year symbolize?

5. Hanbok are traditional Korean _____.

1. Spring Festival or Chinese New Year 2. False 3. Year 4. Abundance 5. Clothing